GOD ALWAYS ASKS THE IMPOSSIBLE

JEAN-JACQUES TRIFAULT

FOOTSTEPS TO WISDOM PUBLISHING

Other books by Jean-Jacques Trifault:

Everything is a Gift
God is in My Heart
Gratitude to the Creation
An Open Heart Comes from an Open Mind
Can We Be the Gift for Someone?
How to Live Life
Among Those Born of Women There was None Greater Than John
The Body of Christ
The Rebirth of God and Lisa
We Do Not Know Ourselves, We Discover Ourselves
(Several books are translated into French and Spanish.)

To order books, please visit the author's website:
www.footstepstowisdom.org or www.amazon.com

ISBN: 978-0984743346

Cover design by Kasia Krawczyk

GOD ALWAYS ASKS
THE IMPOSSIBLE

Humans are mysterious and beautiful beings, extremely sophisticated and complex. We are made in such a way that it is possible for us to receive a multitude of signals within us, through our senses, describing the environment around us and guiding us how to interact with it harmoniously.

We are not the only living beings who can receive signals. Nowadays, we have the privilege to be able to watch many nature shows that reveal the variety and sophistication of the animal and plant realms. We can observe that animals and plants also have some kind of guidance systems that helps them to survive, described as their instincts or reflexes. With the help of these systems, animals and plants can direct themselves to fulfill their important role in the fragile balance of this complex physical world.

Regardless we can be fascinated by the animal and plant kingdoms, if we observe human beings, we can recognize that humans have the most highly developed ability to receive messages and to process them. Categorizing these messages into different scopes or dimensions, we can say the first dimension is connected to our instincts, which means we have an innate guidance system that directs us to nourish ourselves and to protect our bodies from harm. For example, we may sometimes feel, before or in the process of eating, that a certain food is not good for our bodies, and at other times we may feel we need specific vegetables in order to receive certain minerals or vitamins. As well, we sense how we need to clothe ourselves to keep our bodies comfortable and protected from the elements. These behaviors are connected to our instincts, and if we follow those signals then our bodies will not get damaged, but instead we will maintain our health and wellness.

We resemble the animal realm in our reliance upon our instincts, but clearly we also have another dimension that guides us, which is connected to our conscience. In a way, our conscience is like another sense, whose purpose is mainly to promote a character of goodness in us. In accordance with the global purpose

of the human race, our conscience drives us toward the achievement of harmony instead of toward the destruction of each other or ourselves.

If we listen to human beings from various cultures or backgrounds, we will realize that all people receive similar guidance through their conscience. For example, one sentence that all humankind hears is that we should not kill ourselves. This particular voice must be strong in human beings, and because of these words recorded in our conscience, we don't often hear about someone committing suicide. And, if there is someone who hears inside himself the command to kill himself, most of the time he will react by thinking, "This is a bad thing to do," even if he cannot actually find any reason why he should live.

If we wonder why we hear our conscience speaking against killing ourselves or against killing others, it is because inside human beings there is another 'life' or existence, which is connected to the destiny of our souls. Because of the need to develop this other 'life' within us during our physical life here on Earth, we often hear the voice of our conscience guiding us.

However, there have been a multitude of dark times in our history when many people did not listen to the voice of their conscience telling

them not to kill, maybe because they were threatened by their leaders or superiors that if they did not kill, they would be killed. So, in order to protect their own lives, many humans accepted to disobey this specific direction from their conscience.

Even in the worst of times, there was often someone who, in the midst of this pressure to commit violence, would find a way to stand by the voice of his conscience. Perhaps because his conscience became so torn from denying his inner voice, such a person would come to the point of growing tired of obeying his superiors. Therefore, in order to compensate for going against his conscience, he would accept to take the road of his conscience, even to the point where he knew he could be killed by his superiors.

To understand this kind of situation, let us look at the life of St. Paul who, as a Jew and as a Roman citizen, was zealously persecuting Jesus' followers. One day his conscience could not be quiet any longer, and that is when his conversion began to take place. He had been commissioned by the high priest to go to Damascus to help suppress Christianity there. As he approached Damascus, he suddenly saw a blinding light and heard Jesus ask, "Why do you persecute me?" Paul was temporary blinded and was led into

Damascus, where his sight was restored by a disciple of Christ. He was baptized immediately and began preaching, even though he knew that now he would be the one to be persecuted by his superiors.

We can observe the struggle to listen to or to deny the conscience on the larger, societal level as well. When there are many people who do not follow their conscience, if some try to follow it, they will usually be regarded as strange by the ones who deny their conscience. Rivalry can develop between these two groups of people, the ones who have begun to follow their conscience and the others who do not follow their conscience, to the point that one group can feel they have the right to try to eliminate the other group, and large level conflicts or war can occur.

In addition to the struggle historically between these two kinds of groups, one trying to follow their conscience, the other trying to deny it, there have also been individuals who were not just content to follow their conscience, but who felt the call to ascend to an even higher level or dimension of life. We call this, the dimension of emotion or feelings. The reason some people chose to try to enter this dimension is because they had an experience with God's feelings, an experience with love, and due to this they started to want to see an

11

end to the misery of humankind and of God. Although they were often persecuted by those around them, these people accepted to be sacrificed instead of denying their experiences, often to the point of losing their lives. Striving for utmost virtue, these people tried to love the ones who wanted to push them away or kill them, with the words uttered by Jesus, "Forgive them, they know not what they do."

An Experience with God

One such special person in history was Joan of Arc. She was only about sixteen when she testified that she heard voices telling her that she could liberate France. Were these voices from God? Was it He who was calling her to push away the English troops who had invaded France nearly one hundred years earlier? One thing is sure, based on her experience with her voices and her emotional connection to God, she accepted to go to see the Dauphin in order to convey a message to this ruler who later would become the king, Charles VII.

Initially the Dauphin tested her by disguising himself while someone else acted in his place. Even faced with this test, she identified the future king from the crowd and said to him, "I will make you the king of France again."

Regardless this testimony comes from medieval times, I believe today we still hear the voice of our conscience asking us different things. If we start to obey that voice, we will see ourselves arriving at a higher place, physically, mentally and emotionally. And, if we can trust that deep part of ourselves, our conscience, we also will find ourselves able to make miracles, as Joan of Arc did in the land that she felt needed her.

You might object that you hear so much noise and confusion inside your mind that it makes it impossible to hear the voice of your consicence. But if you can achieve a certain level of peacefulness, you may be surprised to hear some words arising from your conscience. If indeed you allow yourself some silent time, you will realize that you do not need to be a special or 'chosen' person in order to receive words through your conscience.

Based on this foundation of calmness, everyone has the capacity to hear this voice, regardless of who he or she is. So, if everyone has the potential to hear her or his conscience, the questions we have to ask ourselves are, first, how much effort do we wish to make to achieve a foundation of peacefulness and second, will we want to follow that inner voice once we begin to hear it?

If we can develop the tendency to obey our conscience, regardless how small a thing it may ask of us, this will attract God to us more often, to the point that He can begin to believe that He can choose us to be educated in His image. As we start to quiet ourselves, we will begin to frequently hear the voice of our conscience.

Our conscience usually asks us to do something according to the needs of our surroundings, which means it asks us to perform actions that demand physical and mental effort. Therefore, some people will choose instead to listen to an extravagant quantity of music, whether it be heavy metal or classical, and others might choose to focus to the television, computer or phone, with the purpose of covering up the voice of their conscience. Because of the strong demands of the conscience, many people have tried to do anything to not listen to it. The practice of being surrounded by noise or involved in a constant flurry of activity has helped many people to avoid the silence that is necessary to hear the inner voice of the soul.

However, when we find ourselves in a place where no music or sound of television or images from computers or phones can reach us, the dreaded moment of silence might sneak up on us and we might be shocked to hear our conscience reminding us of what we should do in that moment.

Live Outside Ourselves

What does the voice of our conscience ask us to do anyway? Regardless we might in that moment object to what our conscience demands, what it asks has the goal of transforming us into someone bigger and more enriched. Overall, we can say that this voice always asks us to help our neighbor or to look at others in a more positive way.

For example, we might hear the voice saying, "Your friend needs something from you." Many times this voice will come just before we finish eating our meal completely or when we finally sit down to rest for a moment. Or, if we plan to go shopping, the voice might say "Why are you going shopping by yourself? Why don't you ask your friend if she would like to come with you?"

Maybe we see a nice piece of cake and we wish to eat it, but the voice might remind us, "You cannot eat it until you invite your friend to share it with you." If we decide to ignore that voice and eat the cake anyway before our friend arrives, we will find that the cake will not taste as good. The reason is because the

joy that arises from sharing cake with a friend will not be mixed in with the cake. Due to the lack of emotion, the cake has less taste. This is not because the food has changed, it is just because we disobeyed our conscience that wanted us to wait for our friend before we ate the cake. Because we denied our conscience, the emotion which was supposed to be produced was not there, therefore the cake didn't taste as delicious as it should have.

Regardless we have many times experienced this kind of simple event like eating cake, if we are sensitive we can perceive that we feel different emotions when we are obedient or when we are disobedient to our conscience. When we disobey this internal voice, we will suddenly feel not as good or we will start to feel disinterested in or distracted from our activities.

What is Freedom?

If we have a chance to discuss our observations with other people, we will realize that there are many concepts concerning the conscience. Some people will say that if we start to allow ourselves to hear the voice of conscience we will no longer have freedom and will be obliged to follow that voice instead of following our own feelings and wishes. Others might ask us how do

we know that what our conscience asks us is good? It is true, if we only look at the moment when our conscience asks us to help with the dishes, we can view it as taking away our freedom because we perhaps already worked for ten hours that day and were about to relax in front of the television.

But if we look from a wider perspective at where this conscience wants to lead us, we will realize that if we can follow this voice, the conscience will actually drive us to the place where we will gain a pleasant character and the people around us will be happy to live with us over a long period of time.

Based on discovering where the conscience wants to lead us, we can say that human beings have the potential to take two very different roads. We have a choice to follow the voice of our conscience or to follow our instincts. If we choose to obey our conscience, many times it will ask us to take the road of restriction, obedience and discipline, which is not so popular in our time. If we choose the call of our instincts, this call will drive us to fulfill any wish we have for ourselves, with the promise of finding freedom and happiness at the end of that road. But we should question, what road brings us to true freedom, or, which freedom will make us really feel free?

17

Looking at our own lives, we are probably aware of having experienced these two distinctly different paths. One is a road that demands that we try to hear our conscience and follow it, and the other is a road that asks us to follow our instincts so we will not hear our conscience and will therefore not have to follow it. In other words, one path demands us to believe in the words that appear from our conscience and follow what we hear, and the other road demands from us to deny what we hear in order to follow our personal desires.

If a person chooses to take the road to follow his conscience, he or she will be guided in the direction of becoming a true son or daughter of God one day, because the conscience always aligns with God's purpose and God's ideal. Due to this close relationship between the God of goodness and the conscience, people often identify their conscience with the word of God. As well, when people do not follow the direction of their conscience they will often identify this event as not following God's will.

God Asks the "Impossible"

Regardless of where the voice actually comes from and how we identify the voice, the question human beings are confronted with is

18

whether we are going to be obedient and faithful to this voice? If we choose to follow our conscience, we should not be surprised to discover that this voice has the tendency to ask us to do something we never did before. In other words, the voice will ask us to do something 'impossible'.

What is interesting is that when we start to gain some experience in following our conscience, we will begin to realize what this voice asks, or what God asks, is to do something to help people around us to have better lives. For example, our conscience might ask us not to drop litter on the street. This is not just because it is bad to throw paper on the street but because our conscience knows that someone will have to pick up that paper and put it in the container created for that purpose.

If we look in the direction the conscience asks us to take, we will realize that the conscience is motivated to love the people around us. So, if one day a person who has the job of cleaning the streets realizes that the streets are staying clean, he will know that it is because all the citizens of the city decided to follow their conscience by putting their trash in the trash can, not in the street. Indeed, if all the people could follow this level of conscience, we could begin to say

this city is a place where people love one another.

Our conscience is connected to the purpose of growing our character of goodness, so if we follow the voice that bursts out from our conscience every so often, we will eventually become more and more aware of the presence of God. Due to our development, this presence of God will become so close to us that we will begin to feel we are in relationship with Him emotionally. At this point we will realize that the road of following our conscience is a ladder going to Heaven.

But if the voice of our conscience comes to us when we are at the first rung of the ladder, we may find ourselves wanting to challenge it, grumbling, "What is being asked of me is not realistic." Because of the attitude that thinks, "God is not like us humans, He does not understand our earthly situation" we will question our conscience, "Why do you ask me something you know I cannot do?" But if we take the road of denying our conscience, we will eventually discover ourselves becoming mad at God.

Turn to God for Help

To understand this conversation within ourselves, let us look again at the moment when God came to Joan of Arc. She might at first have answered with such words as, "Don't You know that I cannot do what You ask because it is too big?" which she perhaps felt was the most humble response. But no matter how she replied, God must have continued to talk to her, even though she believed that it was impossible that she could be chosen to save France. He might have answered, "I understand your situation, but the most important thing you have to know is that I know you are the one most prepared to achieve what I am asking, because you will not be able do it on your own but you will have to turn to Me for help."

Basically what God was looking for in Joan of Arc was that she would be desperate enough to turn and humble herself to God to ask Him what to do every time she found her way difficult. Based on this attitude, God knew that He would be able to guide her step-by-step and at the same time give His strength to her.

In our case, too, God often asks 'the impossible'. For example, to simply smile to a friend is usually not a big deal, but if our conscience asks us to smile to a person we do not like, we absolutely need the power of God to achieve this miracle, therefore we will need to turn to Him.

When a person doubts what he

hears from his conscience, this creates a problem for God as well as for the person, because God is unable to give the love necessary for this person to achieve what his conscience asks of him. This is why God can only hope the person does not abandon Him during the process of following the demands of his conscience. In other words, the person's mind needs to be centered on God, or in the vertical position, in order for God to be able to give His love, which will nourish this person's soul and allow him or her to accomplish what the conscience asks.

In order to help us to achieve that vertical position where we can receive the love of God, God has to ask human beings to do impossible things, like to love our enemies or people different from us, in order for us to turn to Him to help us. God's intention in asking us such impossible things is not that we try to love on our own, but mainly that we accept to humble ourselves in front of God in order for Him to give His love to us, which will enable us to love others.

Regardless of God's intention to have human beings turn to Him when they are asked to do something difficult, human beings usually choose to try to fulfill the voice of their conscience without relying upon God. But the reality is that when people try to do something good without first turning to God, after a certain period of time they come to the point where they realize their investment of love in others is not working and they begin to feel frustrated.

So, if we have a problem to love humanity, especially when we find that people are not responding to our investment in them, God also has a problem, which is to find a way to make people turn back to Him in order to receive His help and ultimately to be able to receive His love.

When Joan heard the voices inside her soul saying, "You are the one who will save France," she must have questioned at first where these voices came from. Surely, if she did not have a concept that God existed, she would have doubted the voices and concluded that the words she heard were lunacy, and would only bring her trouble in the end.

But if she believed that the voices were coming from God, then that idea would certainly have made her want to unite with the God of Heaven, the One who sent the message. The reason she would take this path is because she knew that if she did not keep unity with this God, she would not have the confidence to start nor know how to proceed.

Divergent Roads

We might question whether it is possible for us to take the road of our conscience, which drives us to be good, and at the same time take the road of our physical instincts, and arrive at the same place?

Based on our life experience, we may have already discovered that not every road arrives at the same destination. Therefore, we should want to choose our path well, if we dream to finish our life on the side of goodness instead of on the side of our instincts. If we want to please both sides equally, it would be wise to know that we are not going to end up where we dream to be. Instead, we are going to stay in the same place or regress, regardless of the impression that we work hard and that we become old.

Whatever road we choose, we should know that we are going to have to pave that road with our sweat and hard work every single day. And, whether we choose to believe and follow our conscience or choose to reject the voice of our conscience, we should be aware that we are 100% responsible for our choices.

Although it is the voice of our conscience that shows us the road, it is important to remember it is human beings, after all, who choose the path. Therefore, if someone chooses the path of goodness that brings him in the direction of God's heart, it means this person will totally abandon the road that refuses to be with God. But if we choose the call of our instincts, which demands us to reject the voice of our conscience, this choice will take us on the road to selfishness and away from God.

Even when we know these two different roads will drive us in opposite directions, human beings usually have the tendency to try to compromise. It means that sometimes we will walk the road that asks us to be a little bit selfish and another time we will accept to follow the words that will increase our original nature of goodness. But when these two sides both ask us to achieve more for their own side, we who are in the middle will ask both of them to be quiet. And, if one side still insists on being followed, we will plead, "Don't ask too much of me."

Based on shifting between our conscience and our instincts, we learn to let the two natures co-habit within us. Even though people of conscience pray and do good actions, because they are not absolute and often compromise with the voice of instinct that asks them to be a little bit selfish from time to time, these persons cannot see themselves changing into better people over time.

So, based on the reality that many

people can stagnate, we can recall some words spoken by Jesus, who said that if we don't go forward, we will go backward: "No one who puts his hand to the plow and looks back is fit for the kingdom of God." (Luke 9:62) If we don't promote goodness, the instinct of selfishness will promote itself, step-by-step, until it wins over goodness.

If we look at the lives of some persons portrayed in the Bible, we can say the voice we hear in our conscience is the same voice that Job heard in his head asking him to remain faithful to God, or that John the Baptist must have heard in order for him to accept to go into the wilderness and spend his days praying to God. We can acknowledge it is the voice of their conscience that the ancient sages and monks heard when they secluded themselves in the mountains and the monasteries to find God. Although our life is not as extreme as theirs, we too have to recognize the voice we hear sometimes as the same one that everyone hears at some point in their life, asking them to turn to God and to do something for others.

Obstacles to Following our Conscience

So, if we all can hear the voice of our conscience, which asks us to do something good, why are there not so many people who become good to the point that they can feel God's presence with them?

The main reason is that people try to cover the voice that asks them to do something good for others, until they are no longer bothered by that voice. As they gain experience in covering the voice of their conscience, by blocking it with noise or with a busy lifestyle, they will also start to create a multitude of philosophies or justifications to reject the voice.

Regardless people try to reject the voice of their conscience, an interesting fact is that when human beings start to suffer, especially physically, they have a high tendency to turn to God and ask for some support. However, when they begin to feel better to the point their bodies are comfortable, their bodily instincts demand them to abandon God and ignore the voice of their conscience.

Due to this great possibility for human beings to block the voice of their conscience, we can say that even in the midst of religious people, we still find them doing things that are not consistent with the path of goodness. The main reason is that they lose the discipline to continue to believe in their conscience and to obey it, and therefore they choose to follow their instincts which demand them to follow selfishness through the activities of their flesh.

Due to the fact that we expect a religious person to believe in the voice of his conscience and to obey it, when we see this person becoming selfish and following the instincts of his flesh, we might say about him, "What a hypocrite he is!"

When we start to see religious people acting against their conscience, we usually tend to conclude that the church they represent is corrupt. The real problem is that when religious people's resistance toward the demands of their instincts weakens, they begin to use the word of God to judge others instead of using it to guide themselves. As a result, these religious people actually take the downward road, even though their intention and desire was to grow toward goodness until the end of their lives.

Due to this lack of awareness of the purpose of the word of God, millions of religious people, especially those in the positions of leaders and teachers, decline regardless they constantly preach to their members or to their students to go up. In fact, because they are so busy preaching and teaching to others, they can feel justified in not fulfilling what their conscience asks them to do. Due to this lack of faithfulness toward the voice of their conscience, God cannot help them personally, even though the words they

preach can strengthen many people's belief in God.

Another obstacle to following our conscience is complacency. When we are young, our tendency is to go forward and take on new challenges. But after a while, we are content with what we have achieved and forget that our conscience does not recognize our contentment but will continue to cry out until we fulfill our destiny of divinity.

Therefore, this special voice will continue to ask us the impossible, which means to ask us to believe in something new or to do something that was hard to do previously. For example, we may be a person who finds it hard to open a book containing the word of God, but because we accept to obey our conscience, over time we will find ourselves opening that book every day, eager to read.

Then, after arriving to this stage, our conscience will ask us to achieve another impossible task. This time, God will ask us not to just believe in His words that tell us it is good to love others, but to actively try to love the ones we don't like or the ones who are different from us.

Obedience Leads to Freedom

Why does God always ask the impossible? The first reason is because God knows that if we fol-

low what He asks us to do, we will diminish the power of the 'I' within ourselves, which is sometimes portrayed as our 'ego' or our selfish nature.

Due to God's longevity, He must know what caused humanity to be separated from Him in the beginning, when the ego or the selfish 'I' was introduced inside humanity and became dominant. Therefore, God's utmost desire is to help us to remove the 'I' that demands us to expel everyone around us, including God.

As a first step, God has to teach us to welcome those we find difficult to accept. In order to accept others, God knows we will have to confront the 'I', which is only concerned with 'me', and wants the world to look at 'me', regardless 'I' never look at the world. Therefore, God, or our conscience, will not give us much space to glorify ourselves, but instead will continually ask us to do something for others, regardless we may protest that we already do many things for others. Basically, we can say the conscience doesn't give us any time to enjoy the feeling of accomplishment because it knows an unconditional attitude is best.

Due to the conflict our conscience produces within us, it is highly possible that we will argue with our conscience, "Why do You give me another enemy to love, another impossible thing to accept? Why don't You give me peace now, after working so hard? Do You know, I have have kept faith in You for so many years now?"

The reason we could argue with the One who sends the voice of our conscience is mainly because we have the desire to enjoy ourselves in that moment. But we have to understand that if God starts to hear our protests coming to Him, He will feel sad and might respond, "It is true that you are working hard, My son (or My daughter). It is true that you have kept your belief in Me, and all this foundation is exactly why I am now asking you, instead of stopping at the stage of faith, to love My people."

If we still resist, it is possible at this point that God would ask us lightly, "Should I find someone else?" Feeling a bit shocked, we might respond, "Well, I am not sure, I was just questioning, why is it always me that you ask something of?" And, if God can still feel comfortable with us in this moment, God would respond, "My son (or My daughter), I have already asked many people but they responded the same as you. They asked, 'Why me?' or said, 'What You ask is impossible.' And due to My demands, they left Me and never came back, because they knew I would ask the same

things again, no matter how much time had passed."

Recognizing that God can approach a soul in a private moment, and that human beings can respond to God, we can perhaps understand that when the voice came to Joan of Arc, she could only see herself as a helpless young girl with no power on her own to achieve the incredible task of saving France. But we can question, did God come only to that peasant's daughter who was working in the middle of a field? Or did God first come to the general of the French forces or to the Dauphin himself? Since we never heard about these leaders who governed the land of France receiving a message from God, we can surmise that either God never approached them, or they must have refused to believe in the words of their conscience.

Perhaps, based on their rejection, God was obliged to choose this young maid who seemed to have no means of fulfilling anything God could ask. However, based on her faith, humility, and obedience, God was able to change the path of her land.

Now, knowing that Joan of Arc was asked to do the impossible with the risk of dying every step of the way, perhaps we might re-question, do we like the voice we hear? It has the tendency to follow us everywhere, doesn't it? And, it seems to know what is most difficult for us.

Observing this situation, we might deduce that the One who gives the word through our conscience must be Someone who is watching us from within ourselves, and knows our inner conflicts. Basically, this Voice wants to free us from another voice that accuses us of being bad, which arises from our egoistic nature.

If we are familiar with the other voice that enters our mind, always accusing us of being bad, lazy, hypocritical, surely we wish to find a way to escape from it. But only the voice of our conscience can lead us to freedom from that accusation, if we obey it. Therefore God hopes that He can find, above all, a pure and obedient person.

This is what happened to Joan of Arc. She heard, "Go talk to the Dauphin; ask him to help you to push away the English. Don't worry, I will be with you." Hearing this she must have felt desperate and fearful, and due to this she may have replied to God, "But I don't know anything about warfare, how can I dare to approach the Dauphin?"

Knowing the level of purity of Joan of Arc, God could have answered, "I am aware you don't know. It is because you don't know any-

thing about the Dauphin or the English or warfare, that I chose you. It is wonderful that you are ignorant of these things, because you will not forget to turn to Me, the One who sent you. Due to the fact you have to turn to Me, one thing is sure: you will be able to develop a deep relationship with Me."

Perhaps God continued: "If I choose someone who thinks he knows how to do everything, he will always respond to Me, 'I know, I know, I know'. And, due to his strong 'I', it will be impossible for Me to be with him or to ask him to help with something when I need it. Therefore, I will be obliged to let him to do whatever he wants. But worst of all, at the end of his life, after rejecting Me and continuing to grow his egocentric 'I', maybe this person will come back to Me for help.

Therefore, based on this experience, it is better I choose you, Joan of Arc, because at least you will stay with Me, until maybe the day you will also say, 'I know.'"

How can God Come to Us?

Due to the likelihood of believing that we know when we really don't know, throughout history we have observed the incredible event of God choosing gentiles or ignorant people or even atheists, who could abandon their will because they didn't know anything about God or what He wanted to achieve through them. Due to their open minds, it was possible for God to present Himself the way He liked.

For example, when God chose St. Francis, at that time he was a young, wealthy man who just wanted to enjoy life. But because of an extreme experience that caused him to question the purpose of his life, God could approach him and ask him to do the impossible, which was to give up his way of life and dedicate himself to live with Christ. And in fact, through the testimony of St. Francis, we can see that throughout his daily life he spoke to Jesus as his Lord, in hopes that his new Lord would take his hand to guide him to achieve the many 'impossible' things that he felt called to do.

When we feel helpless to fulfill what our conscience asks us to do, God can begin to be with us. When we have no idea how to move forward, we are often more open and faithful to whatever God demands of us. Therefore, when God asks us to do something impossible, the right mental attitude is not to believe that we already know everything, but instead to accept that God knows more than we.

For example, if our conscience asks us to become perfect as Jesus

was perfect, surely our instincts will tell us, "This request is impossible." But if we look at our innermost heart, regardless this request may look impossible to achieve, we will feel, "This is what I should achieve."

The moment we choose to accept the voice of our conscience, we begin to humble ourselves. When God sees this attitude, He will begin to feel hope, and through this humility we will find ourselves saying, "God, I cannot do what You ask me on my own, but with You I believe I can do it."

Due to the fact that we include God with us after hearing the demands of the voice of our conscience, in this moment God's heart will feel incredible joy and we will also feel so much love coming to us.

But if after hearing our conscience we respond, "Why can't You do the job, God? Why do You need me?" then regardless we try to include God in our thoughts, God will never be with us. This is because God wants to hear, "I need you, God, not to fulfill the task for me but just to be with me when I try to achieve what You ask."

When we invite God to be with us, He feels He can give His love freely. If we say to Him, "Father, I cannot be perfect without You; what You ask seems impossible, but I will try, no matter what, so please be with me,"

36

then He will be by our side twenty-four hours a day if it is possible. He will respond, "Due to your invitation, I can come even closer to you."

To perceive the attitude humans need to have in order to relate with God, we can look at an example from biblical history. When the Israelites left Egypt for the Promised Land of Canaan, they had to leave their homes and walk many miles in the wilderness, which must have seemed impossible to them. Yet to help them, God was walking with them, giving them manna and quail for nourishment, and a pillar of fire and of cloud to guide them. Regardless their plight looked so fearful, God wanted to help His children upon seeing them trying to achieve the impossible task of abandoning their old, selfish way of life and choosing instead to follow Moses and to perfect their character of goodness.

Human Responsibility and the Miracle of God

We can now understand that God asks us to do something difficult in order to help us to become humble, so that He will be able to give His grace to us. As a first step, God asks people to learn to believe in Him, and after this He will ask them to act upon their belief, perhaps saying,

"Why don't you go out and serve people of different races and cultures?" God knows this is impossible to achieve without Him. He knows that if we commit ourselves to fulfill this task, we will need all of God's wisdom and all of His heart to achieve it.

For us to achieve a humble attitude, we will need to become like children in front of God. We know the main characteristic of the mind of a child is to not have much of a concept of what is good or what is bad. This is the reason a child has little difficulty to relate with another child, even if that child comes from a different race or country.

Based on this attribute of children, even though we have become adults, physically mature and well-educated, God still hopes to see us relating with other adults without any difficulties. To achieve that, we have to remove the big 'I' that asks us to only be concerned with ourselves, and replace it with the voice of our conscience, which has the tendency to have a broader view.

If Joan of Arc was just focusing on her 'I' and was not embracing the idea of helping her nation, it would not take too long for her to say to God, "Your idea is impossible to achieve." But because her 'I' must have been weak and her concept of living for others must have been strong, then when God approached her with the idea that she had to help her nation stand up again, she did not feel this was strange but instead she believed that it was possible. To be able to be so positive to God's voice, she must have had a humble heart and a developed desire to help others, in order to believe she could fulfill something she hardly knew anything about.

After hearing God's voice, I believe Joan of Arc must have had a desperate heart and cried many times, eventually calling to her Heavenly Father to give her some details about that impossible mission. Regardless of her desperation, perhaps God only responded, "I don't have any details to give you right now, but you will receive some messages along the way at the right time. And based on this minimal answer, perhaps she pleaded, "Please, You cannot just abandon me like this, how will I fulfill this quest?" But regardless of her wish to know in advance what she would need to do, God answered to the worried Joan, "I will be with you. Please go."

Can we perceive the intimacy of this relationship? Because Joan knew nothing about how to fulfill her mission, she was therefore obliged to depend on God. This dependency allowed a deep relationship to develop between her and

39

God, which would help her through the struggles of her spiritual life as she encountered countless obstacles in the royal court and on the battlefield.

In this modern time, we have adopted the belief that we should be independent from everything and everyone around us, and from God as well. This belief is one of the biggest reasons that we easily reject the invisible voice. Due to the isolation we have chosen, we have no difficulty to consider that others should take care of their own selves, to the point this thought has permeated our society. Based on a multitude of sophisticated justifications, human beings have found the way to isolate themselves from each other, and especially from the presence of God. But regardless that this idea of being independent has been presented as an important step toward adulthood, it is questionable whether this idea really frees humans from their miserable situations.

Regardless of all the philosophies that are created to oppress the voice of our conscience, an amazing point about the conscience is that even if we are at the bottom of a pit of despair, it can still speak to us. And, because of that miracle, we as human beings still have a chance to come out from any imaginable hole or condition we have put ourselves into.

Therefore, there is some hope for human beings, due to our conscience's resistance to dying. If we as humans can come to God desperately, empty-handed, not knowing what to do, this attitude will put us in the right place for God to make a miracle within us. The miracle is that God can tell us something in order to guide us to believe in the right words or to perform the best actions.

Regardless God contributes to making a miracle by speaking to us, the fulfillment of the miracle can only happen when we put ourselves in the position of zero or object under God. Only through our contribution in this way, can God begin to give His energy. Our human responsibility is to find the position of zero, where we actually remove the 'I' whose objective is to reject God. Every time we try to put ourselves in a humble, objective position before God, we decrease the size of the ego we carry, from one hundred percent to ninety-nine percent, then to ninety-eight percent, and so on.

If God did not have much feeling for the human race, surely He would not have planted a 'conscience' in us. But because God does have a plan, which is to be able to give His full love to humans one day, God must wait for human beings to become adults in order

41

to receive His blessing. To achieve this adulthood, God asks us to choose many extreme situations in order to free us from the evil force that has continued to indoctrinate our hearts with its egocentricity.

Therefore, regardless the difficulty, our main responsibility is to choose the voice of our conscience, which shows us the trail we must take to become good persons. Basically, this voice demands the opposite of the voice who asks us to be selfish, and leads us toward the blessing of God's love. We should also be aware, when someone achieves the complete embodiment of selfishness with his mind and his actions, this person also receives a 'blessing' of a different nature from the one who promotes this egocentric philosophy, which eventually manifests itself through depression and heaviness.

Which Destiny Do We Choose?

Although there are some people who choose to be one hundred percent self-centered, there are many who choose to be in the 'midway' position. This means we choose to do good actions sometimes and at other times we choose to do something selfish. Therefore, many people develop some nature of goodness in the midst of their selfishness and are able to keep a

balance between the two sides. Due to this, is it understandable why we don't look too good but not too bad either. Being in this midway position allows human beings to continue to choose between being selfish sometimes and generous sometimes.

Regardless of our view toward this midway position, from the viewpoint of God it is not easy to approach a person who is an expert in staying in the midway position. This is because a midway person will not accept to be disturbed by the voice of his conscience, since listening to his conscience requires a lot of effort. Since many people are in this midway position, where the size of their goodness cannot surpass the size of their selfishness, God finds Himself being rejected every time He asks anything. People in the midway position quickly resort to using an egocentric thought to counteract God's request to be unselfish.

Due to this situation, it is understandable why in Joan of Arc's time the Dauphin and his court did not respond to God, but instead wanted to maintain their midway style of life. Due to their complacency, it was surely difficult for God to find anyone in the court who would work for God's cause. But as well, due to this midway position, it was also difficult for the

side of evil to find someone to completely unite with its idea of creating an egocentric kingdom.

For the devil, similar as for God, to really influence someone to his side, he has to find someone who has a high desire to achieve a totally egoistic way of life. But if every human being tries to stay in the midway position, then the force of evil has to wait until someone wants to distinguish himself by becoming more egoistical than midway people. Only then can evil begin to manifest itself directly through this person and educate him in an evil direction.

Because each human being has individual responsibility to choose his destiny, God as well as the devil has to wait until a person decides whose proposal he or she wants to follow. However, considering both possibilities, we need to admit that the devil has a much easier task of finding someone who can take the absolutely egoistical road, than God who is waiting to find someone who will take the road of absolute goodness.

We can recognize that the force of evil is close to a person when we see someone telling himself over and over that he is a good person, without asking others if they see goodness in him. On God's side it is quite different, because goodness comes not from what we believe but from what we do, therefore God always asks us to do more. God has much more difficulty to find someone ready to follow the road of goodness. Facing such difficulty, God will try nonetheless to find someone who accepts to be educated to take the path where his actions become equal to his beliefs.

In order for God to begin to be present in someone, that person must become absolutely pure or divine. If God can find at least one person among all humanity who arrives at this summit, then He knows that such a person will have the potential to inspire other people to take the path of goodness as well. Until this day comes, God has to continue to speak to the conscience of people, one by one, with the hope that someone will achieve sanctity.

Now that we have become more aware of God's situation, are we going to believe in our conscience and, as a second step, are we going to follow our conscience? Because we as humans are not all at the same place on the road to goodness, each person's task will be different.

Yet wherever we are on this journey, we have to always seek the place where our humility can draw God's love inside of us. If God comes with us we are not alone to achieve an impossible task, and this time we are in the position where

we can fulfill the commands of our conscience.

God's Mysterious Power

Based on knowing it is only when we find some kind of unity with God that we become clear and strong, we can say that no matter how great and how powerful God is and how small we as individual humans appear to be, there is still something mysterious about God's power. God doesn't determine the destiny of the world, even though He is the Almighty Creator and Designer. Despite God's overwhelming participation in the creation process, human beings still have a portion of responsibility for its outcome. It is like God has ninety-five percent responsibility for the outcome of the creation, while humans have five percent responsibility. However, this five percent responsibility represents a human being's full, wholehearted effort. Only when humans unite with God by choosing to achieve the impossible things asked by their conscience will this form the sum of one hundred percent.

If humans accept to recognize God as their Partner in order to fulfill this one hundred percent, this power of unity will begin to influence the egoistical force in us and around us, pushing it back. However, this same equation operates on the devil's side as well. The force of destruction also represents ninety-five percent powerfulness and the self-ish side of human beings represents five percent. Therefore, if the devil can find one person to ful-fill this five percent portion by being absolutely selfish, the sum would allow the power of dark-ness to become one with that person, who would become the manifestation of the Lord of Terror.

If we understand how this invisible equation works, we will be very cautious about what part of ourselves we follow. Do we prefer to stay neutral, happy with ourselves, just the way we are? Or do we prefer to expand our goodness in order that the God of Love can win over the side of our ego?

One thing is sure: if we split our five percent be-tween God and the devil, that will satisfy neither side and will just make us useless for both. So, we must look at both possibilities and decide what we want to do.

Now, are we going to challenge ourselves to accomplish the impossible? How-ever, we will find that if we try to love without God's presence on our side, loving becomes the most frus-trating thing we could ever attempt, especially if we expect someone to change. But if we try to invite God with us as our first priority, every-

thing will suddenly become possible, and when the impossible task becomes possible, we will not want to separate ourselves from God ever again. And, because God sees us depending on Him over and over, God knows we will be able to remove our selfish personality, which is embedded in our instinct, and begin to achieve holiness.

If we look throughout history, we know there were many people who tried to remove their egoistic nature, referred to as sin. But after a while, we usually see little left of their efforts. Based on this lack of substantial result, we could question whether it is even possible to remove our egoistic nature. Is it just a dream that cannot be fulfilled?

Our desire has always been to remove our selfish nature, which is the enemy of love. But what we do not understand is that without God's personal love, we cannot do anything about what we don't like inside of us. Until we begin to humble ourselves before the living God, it is impossible to see a great transformation, regardless we have an avalanche of hope of becoming a great person one day. In other words, if human beings do not humble themselves in front of God before trying to fulfill their desire for goodness, they will just stay passive, in the midway position, or

even decide to act upon their selfishness as revenge for not finding the way to become good.

If we look from a different angle, we can say that the purpose of life in this physical world is to develop our mind and our heart and to maintain our body's purity in order to achieve the dream of our heart. To develop our mind, we need to learn to have faith in the word of God. But to develop our heart, we need to face something impossible in relation to our heart. The main way to strengthen both our mind and our heart is to turn to God. With this kind of attitude of depending on God, God will be very pleased to come and give His love to us, as nourishment. As we receive this ingredient of love from the Source, our souls will be filled up and we will be able to say that we have a heart.

Become a Good Land For God

When God asks the impossible, this demand makes us feel like something inside us is dying. But if we stop our screaming and look at what is really happening, we realize that it is actually our selfishness that is dying when we try to fulfill what our conscience asks. It is actually our egocentric 'I' who is screaming, because God's demands will cause the 'I' to decrease and our goodness to increase.

Because the force of evil is connected to our 'I', the devil will try to convince us that it is impossible to achieve what our conscience asks of us. But in fact it is our selfishness pleading, "You know that if you do what God asks of you, you are going to destroy yourself."

After understanding the root of the conflict that takes place inside us, can we now say that we will welcome what God tells us? Regardless we might conceptually like the idea of God being with us wherever we go, will we feel happy when God tells us what to do? Will we be able to obey the words we hear, or will we try to cover them? The important thing to remember is that in the moment we choose to follow our conscience, we are actually beginning to win over our egocentric nature.

So, what was the secret of Joan of Arc's success? When she heard the words that she was to liberate France, was it because she believed that she could only do it together with God that the power of England started to crumble? Or, was it because she came with an army that the defenses of each city crumbled?

We know that before Joan of Arc came, the people of France were trying for almost a century to push away the English, but with no success. But when God found a

young woman with absolute faith in Him, He knew that whatever had looked rock solid before would begin to crumble, due to her oneness with her God. Even before Joan of Arc arrived to see the Dauphin, many people around the Dauphin had a special feeling about her. They welcomed her not because they were great believers in God but because they felt the power of Joan of Arc's belief.

Her belief in the word she received and her submission before God created so much authority in her that even the skeptical Dauphin and his court were obliged to surrender to her. And, what became an even greater miracle was that the peasants, who no longer had any illusions of being liberated by the Dauphin or seeing the English abandon their country, suddenly wanted to follow and embrace that young woman who had found God.

Just by observing this awakening that was taking place in a nation whose people normally just followed the instincts of their flesh, the enemy became fearful and began to crumble. Therefore, if human beings choose to believe that they can promote the law of goodness, it will be enough to make the ego that lives within each of us begin to worry a lot.

Until that point, the English felt that France was weak in desire,

51

weak in vision and especially weak in its belief in God. They therefore felt they could stay for years, decades, maybe even forever, occupying France without much bother. But what they did not realize was, God was working hard to find a young person capable of believing in Him in any circumstances, without any fear and without compromising. In the moment God found this person, who turned out to be a young woman, God knew that He had already won. Because of her internal victory, and because God educated this young person called Joan of Arc secretly, she could have faith like a rock and burst forward with the desire to complete the victory before ever wishing to take a rest.

If God could not find and create such a kind of person, France would have had to wait for many more years to be free from the invader. From this, we can understand that if someone follows the voice of the conscience and expands goodness inside his or her soul, goodness will also expand in the world.

So, based on a few persons who pioneered the way of faith towards God, do we today want to help the God of goodness? Do we want to fulfill our five percent, representing our whole effort, or do we sometimes wish to live our life in selfishness? To move toward goodness, we have to know that every day we must find a way so that God can come to help us, by desperately following the voice of our conscience.

If tomorrow we see all the believers in God suddenly rushing out to love the impossible instead of singing in the church about the God they believe in, these believers will be transformed, and surely they will no longer be called hypocrites. Instead, they will be called the real children and the image of God. And, as they serve and love people, it will not be difficult for others to believe that love is more powerful than the ego or selfishness.

If we believe and follow what the voice tells us, God can stay with us and we will feel He is our first love. Looking at the quantity of human beings, we can realize that actually only a few people, some of whom are called saints, could walk this road. Based on the difficulty of their path, we can understand why it is said that many are chosen but few can make it.

Therefore, regardless it feels okay to be in a midway place, it will be sad today and for eternity if we find we cannot live in the realm where love is or where God is. To achieve this, we have to make God our first love, which means we will want to tell Him that His wish is our wish.

If God can find someone who

accepts to put God above him or herself, this is more exciting for God than one million believers who always compromise between trying to be good and being selfish. By choosing to follow the voice of our conscience, we are claiming some territory for God to dwell within us, and if we can win, then our body will become a holy land. Based on knowing where the battlefield is, we don't have to look at what others do. We only have to look at what we want to achieve, and through following our conscience we know that our heart will expand.

If I could tell you something personally, I would say I am so grateful to you if you decide to give your land for God can dwell within it. And, if someone observing you says that you look happy, you can respond, "Thank you for your compliment, but I know I still do not have enough victory for God to dwell in me every day," and perhaps that person will decide to take the same road as you did, instead of being jealous of you who met God. Then, through this person's own personal effort, he or she will have a chance to meet the same God you have met.

So, let's declare loyalty toward our conscience, and through this we will win over the selfishness that co-exists within us. Regardless many people try to love others, be-

cause they choose to do it without God, they will at some point find themselves unable to continue. But now we know that with God we can do anything, and eventually we can help to transform people into beautiful princes and princesses, because we know that only with love, can someone grow.

It is the same as with a plant. No plant can grow without water and sunlight. If we try to love without God, we will only become dry, frustrated and empty, and instead of loving people we will start to have resentment against them.

So, in order to learn to approach this invisible God, we can say, "Do you know, I want to follow my conscience, Heavenly Father, but I do not know how to fulfill what it asks of me." If we keep this attitude of being under God when we try to help people, God will be with us.

If we make this effort to stay under God and accept to turn to Him, we are not just expanding our character of goodness within ourselves, we are also decreasing the quantity of selfishness we are born with. And, because the realm of goodness within us expands, it is inevitable that our heart will increase to the point where we can sense God's love.

Due to this evolution, after a time we can say 'Thank

you' to God for asking us the impossible, because we know that if He did not ask something from us, we would stay in our midway position.

In time, based on our contribution to believe in and to follow the voice of our conscience, we will begin to resemble the saints, and eventually the one called Jesus. If we can achieve this level of goodness, surely God will not be sad, but will be happy, because He can love us as He loves Jesus.

Thank you.

www.ingramcontent.com/pod-product-compliance
Lightning Source LLC
Chambersburg PA
CBHW071643040426
42452CB00009B/1743